MEL BAY PRESENTS

Kurt ROsenwinkel trio

EAST COAST LOVE AFFAIR
Guitar Transcriptions

transcribed by Brandon Bernstein
and Matthew Warnock

Analyzed By Matthew Warnock

Edited by Matthew Warnock, Jon Bremen and Ariel Alexander

Layout and Design By Holly Holmes and Matthew Warnock

All solos are for guitar and sound one octave lower than written.

www.kurtrosenwinkel.com

MWJ Productions

1 2 3 4 5 6 7 8 9 0

Table of Contents

Brandon Bernstein

Brandon Bernstein began studying guitar at age 14. At 18, he discovered his passion for jazz and improvised music while attending Berklee College of Music. After a semester of study, Brandon ventured to Montreal, Canada where he studied jazz for the next four years. He received a BA in Jazz Performance from Concordia University in 2003.

Following his studies at Concordia, Brandon was awarded a full scholarship as a graduate teaching assistant at the University of Louisville where he completed his Master's degree in Jazz Performance in 2005. After finishing his Master's degree Brandon was awarded a Teaching Assistantship at the University of Southern California where he completed his Doctorate in Jazz Studies in the fall of 2008.

Brandon writes for Just Jazz Guitar Magazine and Jazz Improv Magazine where he has his own column and submits reviews. Amongst Brandon's other accomplishments, he was invited to present a lecture on the future of music education in Kuala Lumpur, Malaysia at the International Society of Music Education Conference (ISME) in 2006. In 2008 he presented again—upon request— speaking about integrating the creative process in the classroom-at ISME's meeting in Italy.

As a musician, Brandon has performed and/or studied with a variety of well-known artists including Larry Koonse, Pat Kelley, Bruce Forman, Adam Del Monte, Delfeayo Marsalis, Craig Wagner, Terrell Stafford, Frank Potenza, Roddy Ellias, Greg Amirault, Jack Wilkins, Gene Bertoncini, Ben Monder, Charles Ellison, John LaBarbera, Matt Otto, Tim Pleasant, Jimmy Wyble, John Goldsby, Harry Pickens, Remi Bolduc, Sid Jacobs, Walter Smith, Kate Reid, Ambrose Akinmusire, Sam Minaie, Ochion Jewell, and Mark Ferber. Brandon's first album "Solitude" was released in the Fall of 2008.

Brandon is an adjunct professor at Cypress College where he teaches jazz guitar. He gigs regularly throughout Los Angeles.

Brandon plays a Roger Borys B-120 handmade archtop and a Paul McGill handmade nylon (super ace). Brandon uses Thomastik-Infeld strings. His amp of choice is a Clarus 1R through a Raezer Edge speaker.

Brandon currently resides with his wife, Jessica Weinhold, in Pasadena, California.
www.brandon-bernstein.com

Matthew Warnock

Matt Warnock began studying classical guitar at the Royal Conservatory of Music at age 16. After moving to Montreal in 1998 he switched his focus to jazz studies and completed a BMUS in jazz guitar performance at McGill University in 2003. Upon graduating from Mcgill he was awarded a full teaching assistantship to attend Western Michigan University where he completed his MMUS in Jazz Performance in 2005 with a cognate in music theory.

In 2008 Matt was awarded a DMA in Jazz Performance with a cognate in music composition from the University of Illinois where for three years he taught undergraduate, graduate and DMA level studio jazz guitar lessons and coached the jazz guitar ensemble.

Matt Warnock is currently the guitar professor at Western Illinois University where his duties include teaching Jazz and Classical applied lessons, coaching the guitar ensembles and performing in the Hopper faculty jazztet. He is also on faculty at the Interlochen Arts Camp where he teaches jazz guitar lessons, jazz improvisation, jazz rhythm section seminar, the history of the jazz rhythm section and directs the jazz guitar ensemble.

As well as teaching and performing, Matt Warnock writes lessons, reviews and articles for Just Jazz Guitar magazine, Modern Guitar Magazine, the Jazz Guitar Gazette, Jazz Guitar Life Magazine, is a freelance writer with the Hal Leonard guitar department, and is a staff writer for MusicEdMagic.com

Kurt Rosenwinkel

Kurt was born in 1970 in Philadelphia to a musical family. He began playing guitar around twelve years of age after hearing the Beatles album *Sgt. Pepper's Lonely Hearts Club Band*. His first exposure to jazz came from listening to a local jazz radio station in high school. This prompted him to study at Berklee College of music in 1988, until 1991 when he left to join vibraphonist Gary Burton's group. Following the illustrious start, Kurt also played and recorded with other fine jazz musicians including Paul Motian, Mark Turner, Seamus Blake, Brian Blade and Tim Hagans. After moving to New York in 1991, Kurt became a regular on the thriving local jazz scene and played frequently at the famous Small's jazz club. He has won widespread recognition for is innovative playing and was awarded the Composers Award from the National Endowment for the Arts in 1995. Kurt signed with Verve records in 2001 and continues to record with that label today as well as touring worldwide. He currently resides in Berlin with his family where he is the guitar department chair at the Jazz Institut.

The Album

East Coast Love Affair was recorded between July 10th and July 24th 1996 at New York's famous jazz club Small's. The album features Kurt on guitar, Jorge Rossy on drums and Avishai Cohen on acoustic bass. It was recorded and released by the Spanish jazz label Fresh Sound New Talent, which was beginning to feature young and undiscovered talent including Kurt and pianist Brad Mehldau among others. The album was recorded live to allow the spontaneity of the trio to come through on the recording. It consists of six standards and two originals by Kurt, *B Blues* and *East Coast Love Affair*. As standards are the benchmark by which all great jazz musicians are measured, the album is an excellent opportunity to hear the young artist's interpretation and budding personal style.

Kurt's Gear

Currently Kurt is playing on a D'Angelico New Yorker guitar through a Polytone Mini- Brute III amplifier. For his effects board Kurt uses a Boss EQ unit, a RAT distortion pedal, Line 6 Echo Pro/Delay and a Lexicon LXP-1 Reverb unit.

Kurt Rosenwinkel Discography

The Remedy: Live at the Village Vanguard (2008)
Deep Song (Verve, 2005)
Heartcore (Verve 2003)
The Next Step (Verve, 2001)
The Enemies of Energy (Verve, 2000)
Intuit (Criss Cross, 1998)
East Coast Love Affair (Fresh Sound New Talent, 1996)

For the Reader

We the authors would like to take this opportunity to thank you for supporting this work and supporting the work of an extraordinary artist, Kurt Rosenwinkel. We hope you enjoy learning from this book as much as we have enjoyed writing it.

We would also like to take this opportunity to talk a little about the format of the book and the format used in the musical notation. As can be seen in the table of contents, the order that the solos appear is contrary to that in which they appear on the record. We felt that the solos should be presented in order from easiest to most difficult in terms of learning the solo. We felt that this would help enhance the pedagogical aspects of the book and allow the reader a system in which to guide their study.

As well, we have chosen a system of notation that is closer to the American jazz tradition than to the European art music tradition. Each solo is presented with more of an emphasis on flats, both keys and accidentals, than on sharps, unless it was otherwise unavoidable. We have decided to present the musical notation in such a way that allows the reader to both sight read and sight analyse with decreased difficulty. Accidentals are primarily used to reflect the harmony underneath the solo, though there are some instances where this is not the case. In these instances, we have chosen to go against the written harmonic textures to more easily facilitate sight-reading that section of the solo.

We would also like to thank Kurt for his numerous contributions to modern jazz and to the guitar in general. If it were not for his artistic vision, this project could never have been realized.

Improvisation #1 Analysis

Kurt's improvisation on this tune is a great example of getting a lot of mileage out of one idea. Forty of the sixty-four bars on this tune have chord soloing ideas in them. This is something that is not heard of frequently in modern jazz where most players choose single line improvisations over harmonic ideas. Though most of the solo contains voiced improvisation what keeps it interesting is Kurt's inner sense of melody along with his ability to manipulate rhythms in order to keep the listener hooked.

Kurt has chosen to use three basic harmonic concepts in this solo, the first being triads. We can see his use of closed triads in most of the opening half of the solo. As well, he uses spread voicings like the ones in bars twelve and twenty-five. The attention of the listener is certainly captured, but what is even more interesting is how Kurt uses different triads over the harmony to create new and interesting sounds.

Kurt uses the more traditional sounding 1-3-5 triad very sparingly throughout his solo. We can hear it in bars sixteen, thirty-two, thirty-seven, and thirty-nine, though when he uses these triads they never sound plain or boring. This is because of Kurt's use of motivic and rhythmic development as in bars thirty-one and thirty-two, and his strong melodic sense like in bars thirty-four through forty.

We can hear Kurt using a 3-5-7 triad, the third, fifth and seventh of the chord, in bars two, four, nine, twenty-five, thirty-one, and thirty-four (with the added 11th). This helps give the sound of a seventh chord, which is what is happening harmonically underneath the solo, while the use of rootless voicings prevents a clash with the bass player. It also leaves that voice open for other more interesting possibilities.

Kurt also uses triads that come from the scale in which he is harmonizing, such as bars twenty-one, thirty-five, thirty-eight, forty, forty-six through forty-eight, and fifty-four. These triads are diatonic as often as they are not, but the top note, which sticks out most to the listener, is always from the chord scale or a continuation of his developing melodic line creating a unifying effect.

The second harmonic theme that can be heard throughout the solo is known as a shell voicing. These are four note chord voicings with one note missing, leaving a more open sounding chord, but with the harmony still intact. Kurt uses this in bars fourteen (1-3-7 of a Dm7 chord) and fifteen (1-3-7 of a C#m7 chord). These sounds are pianistic in nature but also sit very well on the guitar's fretboard. This shows us that even though we can learn a lot from the study of guitarists, many world-class guitarists take ideas from pianists as well.

The last harmonic idea that Kurt touches upon in this solo is his use of fourth voicings, which are also very common in jazz piano playing. We can hear him using fourth voicings in bars twenty-six, thirty-three, forty-eight and fifty. The reason these voicings are so effective during this solo is because they have a very open sound. Just like the open voiced triads discussed earlier, these voicings help give contrast to the closed sounding triads and shell voicings.

Kurt's improvisation on this tune may sound very simple at the first listen, but when it is put on paper for analysis it is also a remarkably beautiful and intelligent improvisation. Kurt's use of motivic development and mature harmonic sense shines in every bar. Finally, he ends his solo on one of the tastiest licks I've ever heard, and, true to Kurt's nature, it is part of the motivic structure as well as it is slick.

Kurt Rosenwinkel's Solo on the Chord Changes to
Improvisation #1
Little White Lies

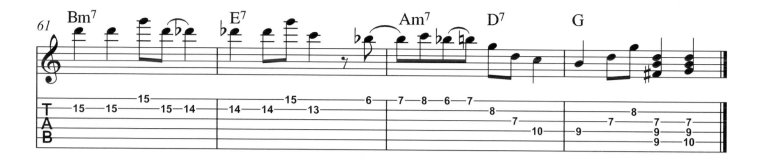

Improvisation #2 Analysis

One of the best aspects of Kurt's playing, which is emphasized in this solo, is his ability to develop motives. We can hear this in his opening line from bars one to three. Kurt uses a descending scale as a melodic motive, which he ornaments by harmonizing the passing chords, while also using a rhythmic motive of alternating groups of eighth notes and a quarter note. Kurt then goes on to further develop the same motive in bars four through six. This time he answers his opening statement with an ascending line that he ornaments and brings out rhythmically. Then just to show he hasn't forgotten his original idea Kurt brings back the same descending motive in bars forty-nine through fifty-three. Only here he harmonizes it with triads and two note voicings, both thirds and fourths. This shows Kurt's maturity as an improviser as he keeps a motive in his head throughout the solo thus giving it a wonderful sense of continuity and balance.

Another motivic idea that we hear in this solo is found in bars twenty-nine through thirty-one and bars forty-six through forty-eight. Here Kurt plays a statement phrase, the descending harmonized chromatic line in the first example and the ascending leaping phrase in the second, and then promptly plays an answering motive after it. In the first example Kurt adds an extra G to the chromatic line and varies the rhythm a bit while in the second line he descends down the arpeggio leading to the E7 voicing, a nice resolution to the line and set up to his next idea.

Kurt's note choices are pretty standard during this solo; he never strays outside the chord very often. One note that he likes to play and is worth looking at is the #7 on a minor chord. This is a result of Kurt's time spent studying bebop, which can also be heard on his great debut album Intuit, because in bebop harmony the #7 is preferred to the b7 on a minor chord, be it a ii or i function. We can hear this sound being used in bars one, two, three, eleven, seventeen, eighteen, nineteen, and fifty-three. In this solo Kurt uses it on the i chord and the iv chord, giving both a melodic minor quality that stands out, especially since he's the only harmonic instrument on the record.

Kurt also has a total command over triads both harmonically and melodically and both can be heard in this solo. We can hear his use of melodic triads in his opening statement with the Am triad and G#aug triad in bar two and three and the Am triad again in bar five. These triads help to give his lines a sense of continuity without getting too complex. It also shows how melodic and hip triads can sound when they are used in this context.

As well as using triads melodically we can hear Kurt's use of harmonic triads in bars nine, fourteen, forty-nine, fifty-three, fifty-five, fifty-six, fifty-seven, fifty-eight, sixty-one and sixty-four. These triads are a great comping tool and show us that Kurt has checked out piano voicings as well as traditional guitar voicings. The triads also add a nice contrast to the fourth voicings, bars twenty, thirty-eight, fifty-three, sixty, and sixty-two, as well as the thirds and sevenths in bars seven, twenty-seven, and forty-one. Kurt also uses partial triads, which are thirds that imply a chord not just a melodic function, these can be found in bars twenty-one, twenty-five, twenty-six and fifty-nine.

Overall this solo contains some great fundamental concepts that show how simple ideas can be developed into a great piece of music. With his use of triads, thirds and sevenths, and motives, Kurt creates a memorable solo that is easily sung back by a listener and readily applicable for the student.

Improvisation #2

All or Nothing At All

14

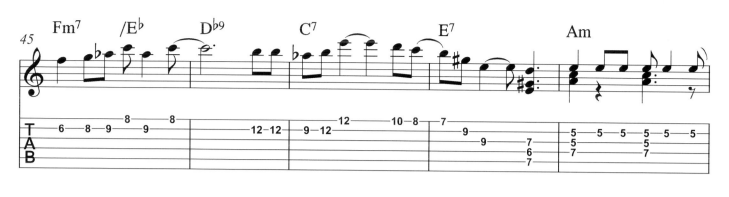

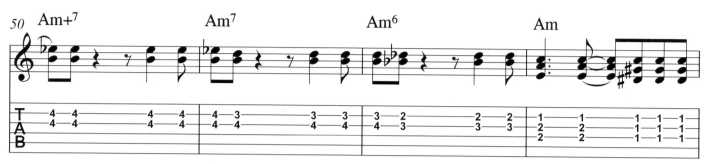

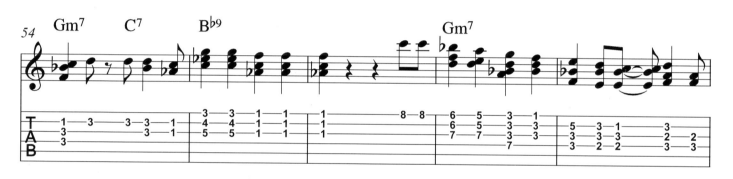

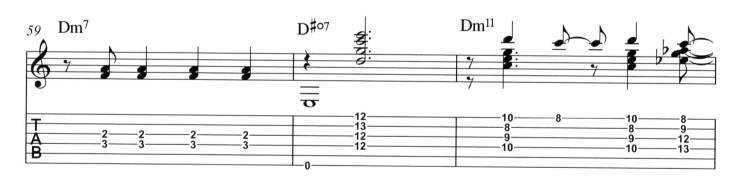

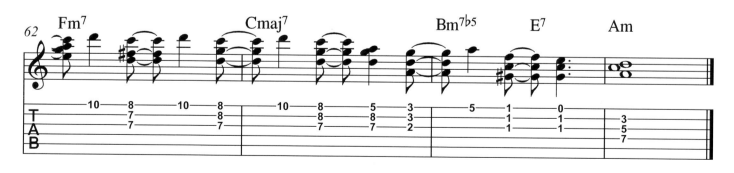

15

Improvisation #3 Analysis

If Little White Lies was Kurt's example of how far one can go with a chord solo, then Pannonica is the same idea, but now with single lines. Kurt uses very few chords in this solo. When he does, their role is that of an accompaniment rather than a melodic role, like in bars eleven, twenty-two, twenty-eight, twenty-nine and thirty-two through thirty-four. Again this is Kurt approaching the guitar like a piano; he uses single lines as the right hand and the chords as the left, something we will see him use at greater length in other solos from this album.

Just like the previous solo, Kurt uses several different approaches to keep the listener interested since he is using only one texture of the guitar for the majority of the solo. If we listen to the solo purely on a rhythmic basis, we notice that he uses all of the rhythmic options he has available to him such as eighth notes, bars thirty-two through thirty-four, triplets, bars eight and twenty-six through twenty-eight, and sixteenth notes, the break, bars three, sixteen, nineteen, and twenty-four through twenty-six.

As well as these basic rhythmic patterns, we also hear Kurt using more complex patterns such as five over one in bars twenty-three and twenty-nine, as well as six over one in bar thirty-four. There is also Kurt's usage of dotted rhythms that stands out in bars three, five, eighteen, twenty, twenty-one, and thirty-one. The dotted rhythms help add a new flow to his lines instead of just swinging the eighth notes as one might expect from these phrases.

The last rhythmic idea that really stands out is Kurt's ability to mix all of these rhythms in a single phrase. We can hear this in almost every bar but some that stand out are bars three, eleven, fourteen, fifteen, eighteen, twenty-nine, and thirty-two. Kurt's ability not only to play different rhythmic ideas, both traditional and modern as well as in any combination at any time, gives his phrasing a unique and distinctive character. These rhythmic ideas help define Kurt's sound and it would be worth the reader checking out these rhythmic ideas in other solos in this book and in other recordings of Kurt's to find additional great examples of these ideas.

Besides Kurt's rhythmic choices, there are other points of interest in this solo that one should check out. The first is Kurt's use of the octave jump as in bars six, ten, sixteen, and twenty-seven. This is a great way for Kurt to shift his lines into different octaves without the need to fill all the space in-between. These octave jumps keep his melodic and linear thought intact while also creating new interest.

Kurt's use of the bebop scale shows us that he has spent his time studying the origins of his art. We can hear this scale in bars three (Ab G Gb), nineteen (F E Eb), and twenty-five (G Gb F). In two of the three examples, Kurt uses the stock root-7-b7 scale which is much more common than the third example where Kurt uses 9-b9-root. Kurt illustrates for us the standard bebop scale with the added 7th as well as the less common bebop scale with the b9. Though not shown here, I would bet he also uses this scale with the b3, b5 and b13 as well.

The last idea that stands out in this solo is Kurt's ability to end a line and while still holding the final note, begin his new line, an idea that is common to pianist Brad Mehldau's playing. This can be heard further in bars fifteen, eighteen and twenty-six. It is a sly way to add different textures to single line playing without actually playing harmony, or octaves, or anything else, for that matter. It is just one more example of Kurt's penchant for studying pianists.

Improvisation #3

Pannonica

Improvisation #4 Analysis

In the solos we have heard so far in this book, Kurt has focused mainly on one idea on which to base his improvisation. In this solo, however, Kurt displays the ability to use his complete pallet of ideas without causing clutter or disorganisation.

The first thing we hear that stands out is his ability to mix rhythms. We can hear this in bar one where he plays on the off-beats, in the third bar where he mixes eighths, sixteenths and eighth note triplets all in the same bar, and in bar fifteen where Kurt plays a sweeping arpeggio lick that is based off of five notes against one beat. Kurt's penchant for triplets shines in bars ten, eleven, twenty, twenty-one, thirty-two, thirty-six, and thirty-eight. Kurt manipulates triplets with ease playing them straight up, with ties and rests, or with different groupings of notes.

Kurt also uses a wide variety of harmonic devices in this solo. He uses triads in bars one, twenty-four, thirty, thirty-nine and forty. Again as in previous solos Kurt uses the diatonic triad, 1-3-5, the 3-5-7 triad and other triads from the scale. Something we haven't heard in previous solos is Kurt's use of triads over a bass note in bars twenty-five through twenty-eight. Here Kurt uses a Major triad over a base note a fourth away. As a result, in the first chord we have an Emaj triad over an A bass, then in the second we have Dmaj over G, and Ebmaj over Ab etc. This is a really nice sound and is easily played on the top four strings of the guitar. It yields yet another side to the simple triad that helps Kurt keep his ideas both fresh and easy enough for the listener to follow and the student to play along.

As well as using triads, we can hear Kurt using thirds and sevenths to comp for himself in bars six, seven, nine and sixteen. We also hear Kurt using fourth voicings in bars twenty-three, thirty-four and thirty-nine.

Kurt shows us another side to his harmonic playing in his use of thirds when he's harmonizing a line. This idea can be heard in bars twenty, twenty-one and thirty through thirty-three. This is a nice way to add some beef to a line without getting too complicated both harmonically and technically. It also gives contrast to Kurt's other chordal lines, which have more than three notes in them and allows for his triad lines, which he is fond off, to sound fuller in contrast as well.

As well as playing nice harmonic ideas in this solo, Kurt plays some very nice melodic lines. His double time lines in bars twelve through fifteen and seventeen through nineteen are definitely worth close study as they fit fluidly on the guitar and are mostly diatonic to the chord changes, fitting for any level of player.

We also hear characteristic motivic ideas in bars six through eight. Here Kurt states his melody then develops it through the second bar and then completes the idea in the third. It's a call and response line with a stretched middle section, adding a little more length to the idea. Kurt also plays and develops a rhythmic motive in bars thirty-six through thirty-eight. Again Kurt states the idea in the first bar, then this time he lets in breath in the second, before resolving it in the third.

This solo is a great example of using many different harmonic and melodic ideas to keep a solo interesting without sacrificing focus. It should be studied as much for the colors used as for the lines drawn.

Improvisation #4

Turn Out the Stars

(1:18)

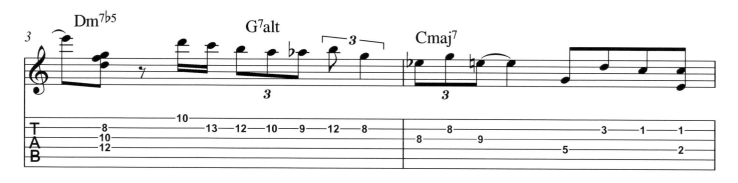

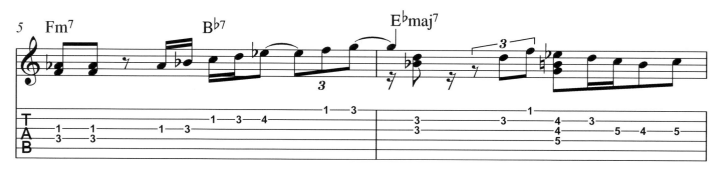

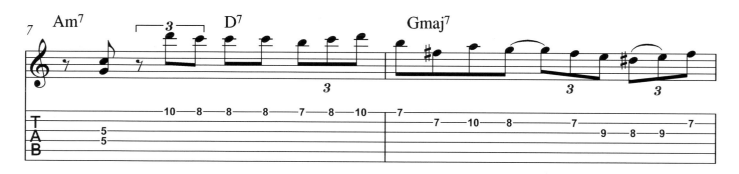

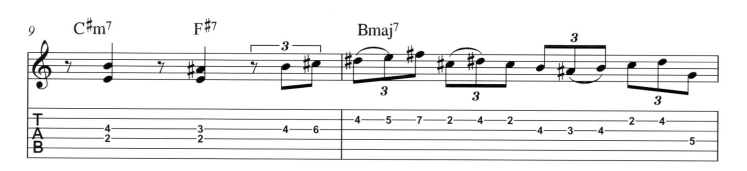

Improvisation #5 Analysis

Lazy Bird is one of the faster solos on this album and this gives us a taste of Kurt letting loose. We can still hear all the wonderful Kurt-ism's such as triads, thirds and sevenths, fourths, and rhythmic ideas. Though Kurt's treatment of these concepts is far more evident on this tune, especially with his ability to play over the bar line.

Even on the first listen, the outstanding section of the tune is bars sixteen through twenty-four. Here we have one of the nicest lines on the whole album and a wealth of ideas in which to take and adapt to our own playing.

The first thing that stands out is the rhythm. Every note Kurt plays during these nine bars is a quarter note on the offbeat, with no resolution to a downbeat even at the end of the phrase. This gives the phrase a feeling of elasticity that pulls the listener to the offbeat, perhaps even disguising the offbeat as the strong beat because of the length of the line.

Melodically, we have a very interesting motive that is being stated, developed and finally resolved during this phrase. The melody is a seven note group that consists of a major third down, minor third up, tone down, minor second down, minor third up, tone down, tone up and a semi tone up. As you can see, this is a complex line that Kurt chose to develop and yet he transposes it up a semitone so seamlessly in the mid-section of the phrase that it seems as though it is part of a composed melody rather than an improvised line. The line is then resolved with the same rhythm only this time bringing us steadily downward to the final notes.

Harmonically this line is no less interesting as Kurt uses substitutions and a variety of voicings to enhance the melodic and rhythmic content of the line. When we look at the voicings separately from the melody line, Kurt's thinking becomes clearer. We can see that he is mainly sticking to triads, both major and minor, with a few fourth voicings thrown in to mix things up. This use of triads enables the listener to follow along fairly easily. Once we are following, he whisks us in and out of the given harmony, all without leaving the contour of the line or losing the listener along the way.

This phrase shows off all of Kurt's strengths while building intensity and interest at the same time. Remarkably, later on in the solo, bars seventy-nine through eighty-two and eighty-four through eighty-six, Kurt revisits the line and further develops it not once but twice. This shows that Kurt never tosses off an inconsequential idea, but rather that he is always aware of what he is playing and what he has played, allowing him to refresh upcoming ideas and weave consistency throughout the entire solo.

Finally, attention should be paid to two very nice single line sections. The first is in bars forty-nine through fifty-four and sixty-one through sixty-four. These two bars mix a triplets in with eighth and sixteenth notes, aptly illustrating how to add rhythmic interest to a line. It also adds intensity and keeps the listener guessing as to what will come next.

The other melodic idea is a motive in thirds that Kurt states for the first time in bar forty-four. This little idea then comes back in bars fifty-eight and fifty-nine, sixty-nine and seventy-six. Again this is a great example of how Kurt keeps an idea going not just through a line but also through an entire solo. Kurt's creation here proves that artful composition can be spontaneous, and thus he produces a work, not just a solo.

Improvisation #5

Lazy Bird

27

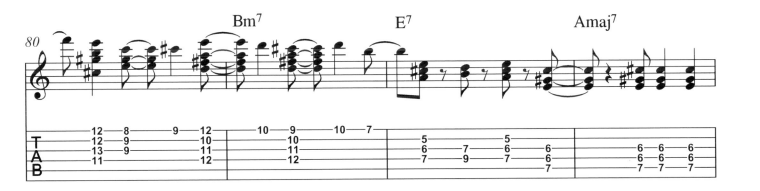

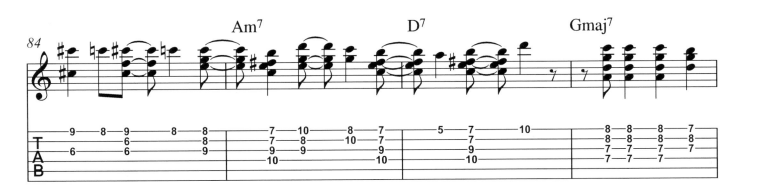

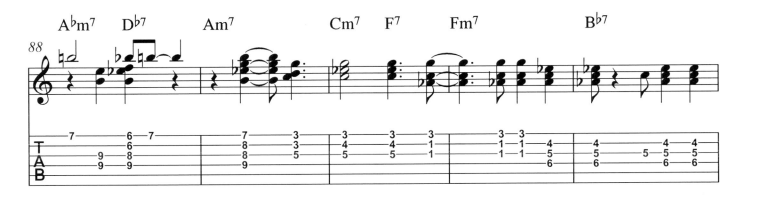

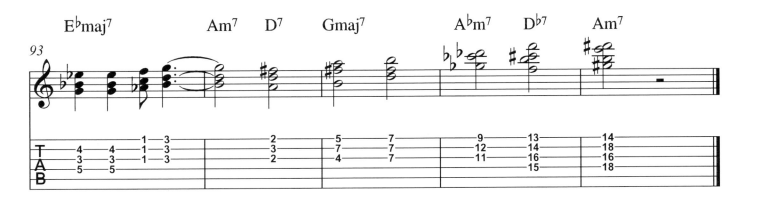

This page has been left blank to avoid awkward page turns.

Improvisation #6 Analysis

This solo is one of the slowest on the album and is definitely one of the busiest. In contrast to other solos on this album, Kurt chooses to hold a lot of his notes for longer lengths rather than let them go and leave the space as is his usual habit. This does not detract from the artistry of the improvisation as the listener hardly notices that there are notes ringing 99.9% of the time. This is the beauty of Kurt's melodic style, it allows the listener to get lost in the content and not focus on how many notes are being playing or how fast they are or how high; rather, it is always about the melody.

There are a few new ideas here as yet unheard in Kurt's previous solos. The first we'll touch on is Kurt's use of leaps, which I will define as an interval of a fourth or further. We can hear lines that have obvious leaps in them in bars one, eleven, twelve, fifteen, twenty-five, twenty-seven and twenty-eight. As well we can hear how Kurt mixes up leaps and arpeggios in lines like bars eight and twenty-two. These leaps add a nice contrast to Kurt's scale based lines and also allow him to cover a lot of fret space as most of these lines cover two octaves or more.

Kurt's sense of melody is heard right away in the opening line based on the blues sounds. Not only does Kurt give us a tasty opening phrase, he then resolves it with his jazzier line in bars two and three. This is a nice set up to Kurt's quote of the melody in bars three and four. Though the quote is indirect and there are many embellishments that add a personal touch to the original melodic line.

As well as quoting the melody Kurt develops motives of his own like the one heard in bar five. This little four note harmonized line is then repeated in bars fifteen and seventeen, again giving continuity to the solo as a whole. The other motive that Kurt develops is initially heard in the first two beats of bar twenty-two. This idea is then altered slightly and repeated in the last two beats of bar twenty-six.

We have seen throughout this book how Kurt has learned from piano players, and in this solo we can see how the great guitarist Joe Pass has rubbed off on him too. We can hear Joe's influence on Kurt in his use of alternating melody notes with chords. This is heard in bars five, six and nine. It is a nice guitaristic approach to harmonizing a line that shows us the diversity of Kurt's influences and how he has taken a traditional player's idea and made it his own in a modern context.

We also have examples of odd groupings of notes found throughout this solo. We can hear them in bars thirteen, fourteen, twenty-one, twenty-two, and twenty-six. These lines add variety to the stock sixteenth note double time lines normally played on a ballad of this nature and also build intensity through rhythmic diversity.

The last section of the solo we will touch on is the final three bars. In these three bars there are many things happening that are worth dissecting. The first is the counter line melody that opens bar thirty-one. The line is fascinating because not only does Kurt add the scale line below the Bb being held on top, but he also has the presence of mind to add a leap at the end that implies the cadence in the chord changes. This is followed by a great us of space that sets up a group accent on the three note chord before resolving down to the triad. It is also a pleasing section of the tune because it shows how the group is constantly listening to each other and playing off of each other. Even though Kurt is improvising, no player is really singled out; they are all making the music together.

Improvisation #6
Round Midnight

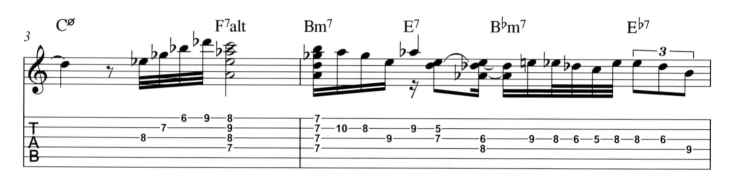

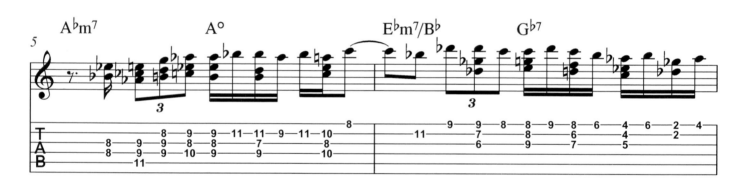

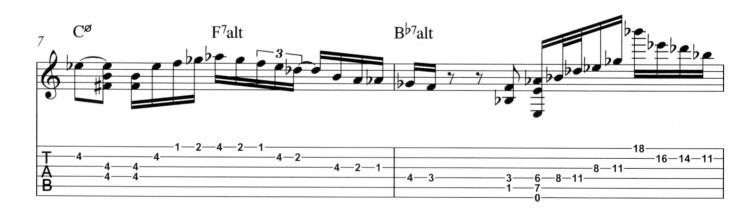

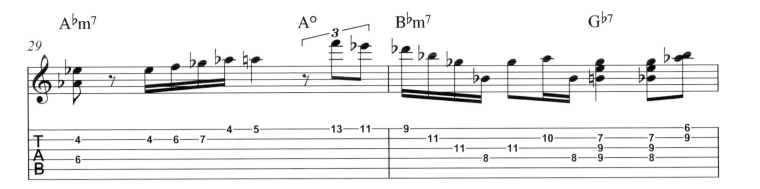

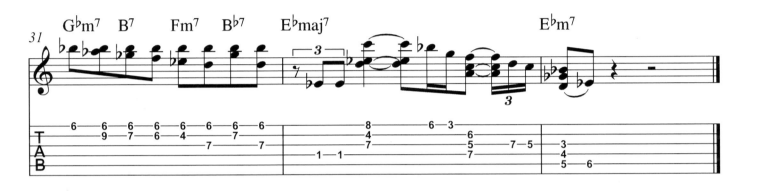

East Coast Love Affair Analysis

East Coast Love Affair is one of the most interesting solos on the album. The tune was written by Kurt and is based on an odd form and a non-traditional chord progression. The solo is thirty-four bars long and is divided into A (8 bars), A' (8 bars), B (8 bars) and A''(ten bars). As well A'' can be divided into two sections of five bars with the first five bars based off of the A section while the last five are new material.

Kurt leans heavily on scale and arpeggio patterns throughout this solo. We can hear examples of this in bar two where Kurt plays a four-note pattern over the D chords with many chromatic notes thrown into the scale. In bar seven, Kurt uses a similar pattern that applies chords to add emphasis and help break up the single note line. This pattern also involves the A Lydian scale with added chromatic notes that help lead into the next chord change.

As well as playing scale patterns Kurt also uses several nice melodic patterns that make these difficult chord changes sound very simple and musical at the same time. In the second half of bar thirteen and first half of bar fourteen, we hear an intervallic idea that Kurt develops over the two different chords. This pattern is especially nice as it uses rhythmic variation to help further this idea that also ends a longer line that begins in bar twelve. We can also hear these melodic patterns in the double stops Kurt plays in bars seventeen through eighteen and the intervallic lines that Kurt finishes his solo with in bars thirty-three and thirty-four.

Kurt does not shy away from using his technical facility throughout this solo. With the slow tempo, Kurt chooses to play longer and faster lines than we have seen in the medium and up-tempo tunes like in bars sixteen, twenty, twenty-one, twenty-four through twenty-six and thirty through thirty-one. These lines vary in their content as we hear Kurt using scales, arpeggios, intervals and chromatic ideas throughout. Even though Kurt is playing longer and faster lines, he never reverts to clichés in his ideas and continues to invent in the moment with the band, not with worked-out material.

This solo shows Kurt using the entire form as his pallet, rather than just improvising on two or four bar phrases. The solo flows nicely from one phrase to the next and each phrase is related to the previous and next lines Kurt plays. It shows us how Kurt can hear ahead of his playing. He is always keeping in mind what he has played and is making a conscious effort to apply what he has played to what will come. This is a quality that all great improvisers have and it is a leading reason why Kurt's solos are so memorable.

Kurt Rosenwinkel's Solo on the Chord Changes to

East Coast Love Affair

(2:35)

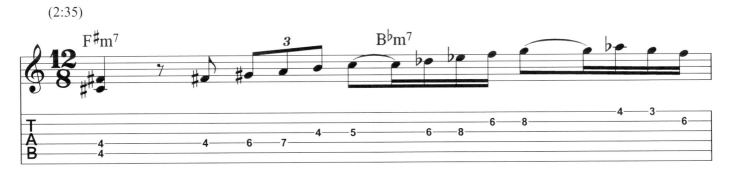

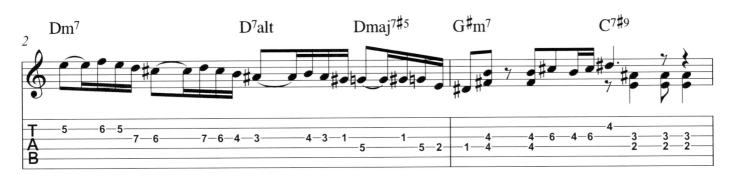

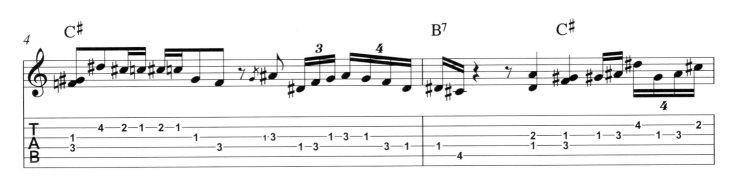

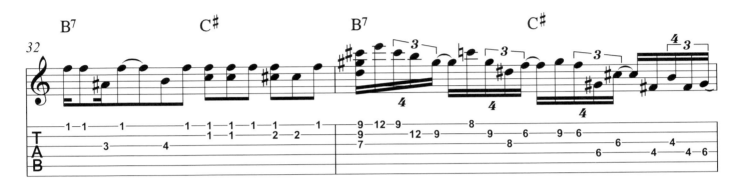

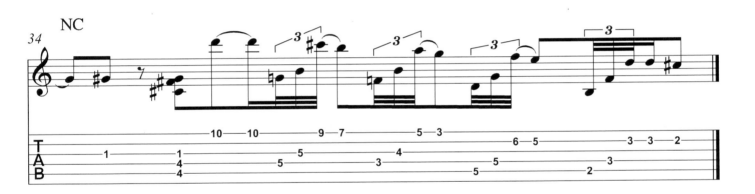

B Blues Analysis

In looking at B Blues, we can divide the analysis into three sections: harmony, melody and form. The solo is divided into three sections as follows: A (twenty-one bars), A (twenty-one bars), and the coda (four bars), with each A section being subdivided into three sections of four, six and eleven bars respectively. The first and third sub sections of the A section start off with the same progression but then Kurt develops the progression further in the third sub section. As well the coda has the same chord progression as the four bar sub section of A.

Kurt's chordal playing is similar to what we've heard in the other transcriptions. In this solo we see Kurt favoring a 3-7-root voicing for the D7 chords, as in bars one, just 3-7 in eleven, thirty-two, forty (substituted over a Gmaj7 chord), and finally over D7 again in bar forty-three. This small three-note voicing gives Kurt the ability to use it percussively as the tri-tone and upper cluster are similar to the voicings used by Bebop pianists.

Kurt uses this percussive approach to the chords throughout the piece as he doubles up on many chords with various eighth- and sixteenth- note combinations. We can hear examples of this in bars one, two, seven, eight, ten, eleven, twelve, thirteen, sixteen, twenty-five, thirty-five, forty-two, forty-three, and forty-four. These repeated chords are sometimes used to set up a single note run which is a nice effect as the listener is drawn to the chord and then surprised with a fast lick as in bars one, eight and eleven.

We also hear Kurt using piano shell voicings in bars two, three, five, twelve, fourteen, fifteen, sixteen, twenty-five and thirty. These shells consists of the root, the third and seventh of the chord to which it implies. This may not always be the chord that is being sounded as in bar three where Kurt plays an Em7 shell over a Gmaj7 chord, implying a G6 sound.

Kurt also uses different secondary triads throughout the solo as in bars twelve, thirteen, sixteen, eighteen, twenty-five through thirty, thirty-four, thirty-five, forty-one, forty-two, and forty-five. These are a nice contrast with the other voicings. The stacked thirds sonority is so common to the listener's ear that Kurt can use it as he pleases like the A triad over Amaj7 in bar fourteen or like the D triad over A7 in bar twenty-seven.

The last harmonic idea we hear Kurt using is stacked fourths. These open sounding chords can be heard in bars two, thirteen, fourteen, sixteen, seventeen, twenty-five, twenty-six, twenty-eight through thirty, thirty-two, thirty-four, forty-three and forty-four. These voicings help contrast the triads as they sound more open ended to the ear and though they imply chord qualities it is subtler than the shell and triad voicings.

Kurt starts his solo focusing on single line ideas before he shifts focus to the previously mentioned chords. His lines are mostly arpeggio based as in bars three, four, five, six, eight, nine, eleven and thirteen, though Kurt also uses scale ideas in bars six, seven, twenty-two and twenty-three. Kurt is a master at mixing scales and chord tones when outlining the chords of a tune, for example, in the Gmaj7 he outlines in bar three and the G7 he outlines in bar thirteen.

Overall, this is the most difficult transcription to perform from the album. It is an excellent study in precise technique and rhythm as well as masterful phrasing.

B Blues

(2:35)

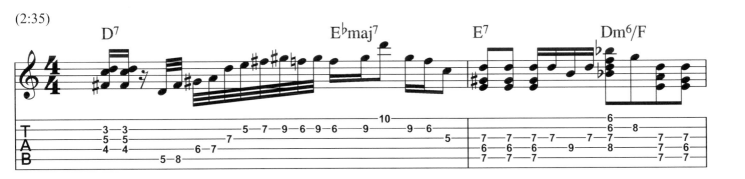

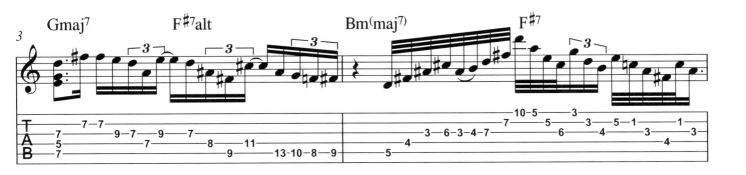

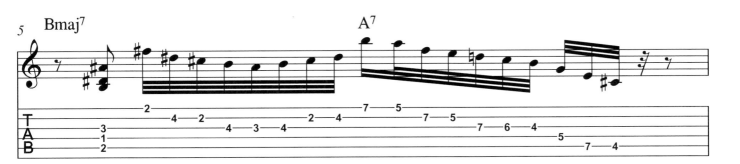

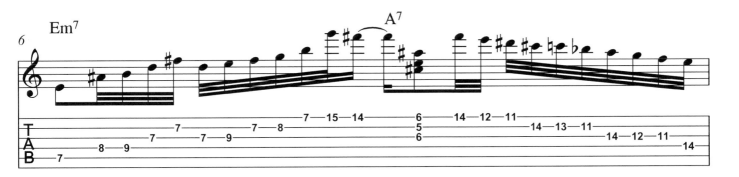

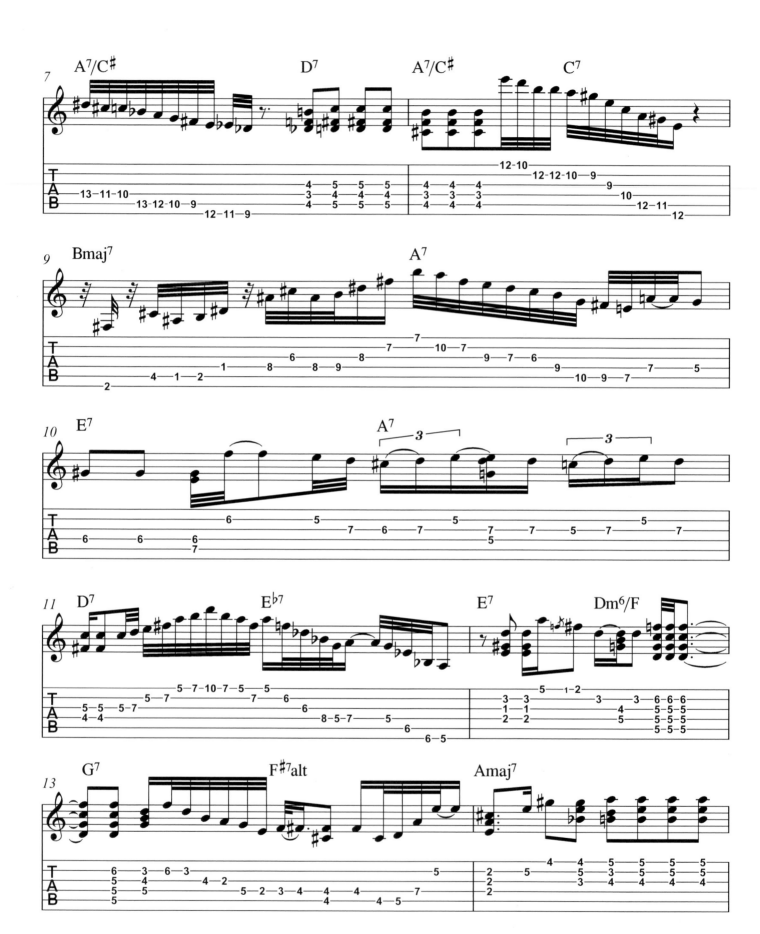

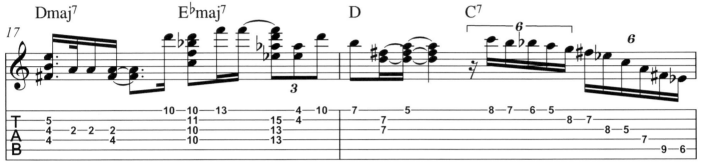

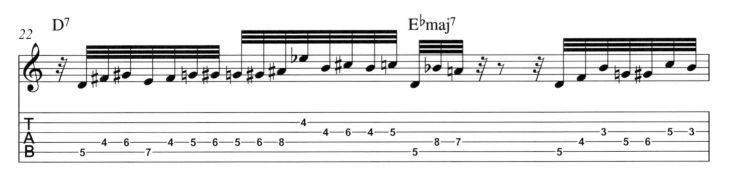

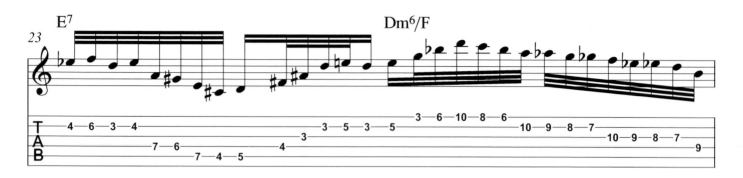

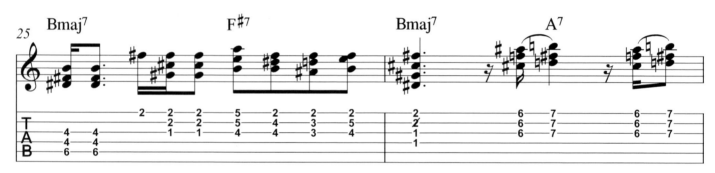

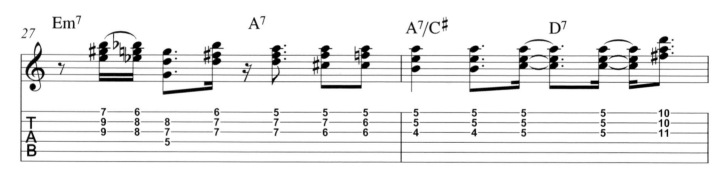

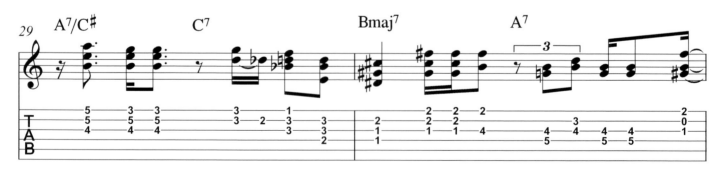